The Promise of New Life

Lent & Easter
with Pope Francis

Amette Ley

*All booklets are published thanks
to the generosity of the supporters
of the Catholic Truth Society*

CATHOLIC TRUTH SOCIETY
PUBLISHERS TO THE HOLY SEE

Contents

All rights reserved. First published 2018 by The Incorporated Catholic Truth Society, 40-46 Harleyford Road London SE11 5AY Tel: 020 7640 0042 Fax: 020 7640 0046. © 2018 The Incorporated Catholic Truth Society.

ISBN 978 1 78469 556 9

SEASON OF LENT

Ash Wednesday

Grant, O Lord, that we may begin with holy fasting this campaign of Christian service, so that, as we take up battle against spiritual evils, we may be armed with weapons of self-restraint. Through our Lord Jesus Christ, your Son, who lives and reigns with you in the unity of the Holy Spirit, one God, for ever and ever. Amen.[1]

It is significant that our journey through Lent is described by the Church as a "campaign" in which we "take up battle" and are required to be "armed" with "weapons". This is the language of warfare and strife; it is not comfortable to hear or to contemplate.

Pope Francis is aware of this as he notes the setting of the first reading – a time of trouble in which the locusts infesting the land are representative of sin and evil which are the true enemy of mankind.

"The Lord alone can save us from the scourge and it is therefore necessary to entreat him with prayer and fasting, confessing one's sins."[2]

The enemy, then, is not necessarily external, though we are often troubled by attacks from without. The real enemy is within us and our repentance and observation of Lenten penances must "transcend mere words or external gestures and elicit true contrition for sin and commitment to keep God's laws."[3]

Pope Francis notes here that the priests of the time had a particular role to play; it is they who are to implore God with tears to spare his people and not allow the nation which should shine like a beacon in witness to become a byword for shame. "Where is their God?"

The psalm which responds to this passage returns again and again during Lent. "Have mercy on me God…wash me from my guilt…cleanse me from my sin…a pure heart create for me…" Our spiritual battle is against sin, against our own weakness, against our unwillingness to put the things of God before the pleasures of the world. The imposition of ashes is a sign for ourselves and for others that we are willing to reverse this, to fight against the temptation to put ourselves first and to be reconciled to God. Pope Francis reminds us that "Reconciliation between us and God is possible thanks to the mercy of the Father who, out of love for us, did not hesitate to sacrifice his only begotten Son."[4]

This may seem a formidable task as we step into the Lenten season, but "In him", the Holy Father points out, "we can become just, in him we can change, if we accept the grace of God and do not allow this 'acceptable time' to pass in vain."[5] And St Paul reminds us "not to neglect the grace of God that you have received". In another translation this is also emphasised: "...we entreat you not to accept the grace of God in vain." We have, through our Baptism and Confirmation and our reception of the other sacraments, especially the Holy Eucharist, *already received* the grace of God. Let it not be in vain.

With the Gospel passage, Pope Francis points out that, when Jesus mentions the three penances of almsgiving, prayer and fasting, he is not pronouncing a new custom but reiterating what was already taught in the Old Testament.

> Do good, and evil will not overtake you. Prayer is good when accompanied by fasting, almsgiving, and righteousness. A little with righteousness is better than much with wrongdoing. It is better to give alms than to treasure up gold. For almsgiving delivers from death, and it will purge away every sin. Those who perform deeds of charity and of righteousness will have fullness of life; but those who commit sin are the enemies of their own lives. (*Tb* 12:7-10)

Jesus takes this practice, well known and accepted by many, and transforms our understanding in his emphasising the essential interior conversion of the heart. Ashes on our foreheads, almsgiving, prayer and fasting, even undertaken in secret, will not help us become reconciled to God without this interior conversion.

Interior repentance is a radical reorientation of our whole life, a return, a conversion to God with all our heart, an end of sin, a turning away from evil, with repugnance toward the evil actions we have committed. At the same time it entails the desire and resolution to change one's life, with hope in God's mercy and trust in the help of his grace. (*CCC* 1431)

As we undertake this spiritual battle, this journey towards the joy and hope of Easter, Pope Francis calls upon our Blessed Mother to accompany us:

> May Immaculate Mother Mary, without sin, sustain our spiritual battle against sin, accompany us at this acceptable time, so that we may come together to sing of the exultant victory on Easter Day.[6]

Challenge: Explain to someone why you need to go to Mass today, or what the ashen cross means.

FIRST SUNDAY OF LENT

They will fight against you but shall not overcome you, for I am with you to deliver you – it is the Lord who speaks.

You shall not fall a victim to the sword: your life shall be safe, for I am with you to deliver you – it is the Lord who speaks.[7]

Today we notice how Pope Francis reminds us of the nature of Lent as a time of struggle and conflict.

"The Church reminds us of that mystery at the beginning of Lent, so that it may give us the perspective and the meaning of this Time, which is a time of combat. Lent is a time of combat! A spiritual combat against the spirit of evil."[8]

However, the Church's message is always one of hope. Even as we are preparing to step into the desert where warfare is threatening and hardships are accepted, we are urged to keep our eyes 'fixed on Easter', to remember that the war against evil is already won and the victory over death is already achieved through Jesus.

And while we cross the Lenten "desert", we keep our gaze fixed upon Easter, which is the definitive victory of Jesus against the Evil One, against sin and against death. This is the meaning of this First Sunday of Lent: to place ourselves decisively on the path of Jesus, the road that leads to life. To look at Jesus. Look at what Jesus has done and go with him.[9]

Jesus has gone before us into the desert; he has suffered all those torments which the desert brings. He has experienced hunger and thirst and the temptation to take a short cut to feed his hunger. He has suffered the loneliness which the desert brings and the temptation to make himself known and revered by people by a show of power. And he experienced the temptation to engage in an agreement with the devil, to take another short cut in order to gain worldly power quickly. We too suffer all these temptations, but we remember the words of Jesus when he referred to the devil as a liar. He "has nothing to do with the truth, because there is no truth in him. When he lies, he speaks according to his own nature, for he is a liar and the father of lies." (*Jn* 8:44)

Once we understand this, we are strengthened to resist our own temptations, both those which we suffer frequently and those extra temptations to abandon our Lenten resolutions. The devil is a liar and those thoughts which we entertain of failure and despair, or of short cuts to glory through cheap grace are lies and will bring us no relief from the desert. The only thing that will make the desert both bearable and profitable during Lent is the presence of Jesus there with us.

The version of the temptations given in St Mark's Gospel is briefer, but we do well to remember these forms of temptation described in the other Gospels as we step into the heat of the desert.

> Jesus decisively rejects all these temptations and reiterates his firm resolve to follow the path set by the Father, without any kind of compromise with sin or worldly logic…Jesus…does not dialogue with Satan, as Eve had done in the earthly paradise. Jesus is well aware that there can be no dialogue with Satan, for he is cunning… That is why Jesus chooses to take refuge in the word of God and responds with the power of this Word. Let us remember this: at the moment of temptation, of our temptations, *there is no arguing with Satan*. Our defence must always be the Word of God! And this will save us.[10]

It is not insignificant that we hear of the covenant of God with Noah and his family at this point in Lent. Noah evidently lived in a world of sinfulness and corruption which the Scriptures link definitively with the physical evil of the flood which swept so many away. It is hard for us to see the connection sometimes, but we also live in a world where those in power, whether material, political or spiritual, have sometimes listened to the devil's lies, become corrupt and sought to pervert others from the path of life. Our hope is in the promise of God; when we see the rainbow we are to remember God's love and faithfulness to his people and also our own Baptism through which we are enabled to enter the kingdom of God. This is our sign, the sign of the promise of life which is ours through our Baptism.

> God's patience waited in the days of Noah, during the building of the ark, in which a few, that is, eight persons, were saved through water. Baptism, which corresponds to this, now saves you, not as a removal of dirt from the body but as an appeal to God for a clear conscience, through the Resurrection of Jesus Christ, who has gone into heaven and is at the right hand of God, with angels, authorities, and powers subject to him. (*1 P* 3:20-22)

Challenge: Explain to someone the meaning of the rainbow for Christians.

SECOND SUNDAY OF LENT

Bless your faithful, we pray, O Lord, with a blessing that endures for ever; and keep them faithful to the Gospel of your Only Begotten Son, so that they may always desire and at last attain that glory whose beauty he showed in his own Body, to the amazement of his Apostles. Through Christ our Lord. Amen.[11]

At this point in Lent we may be feeling the beginnings of tiredness and extra temptations. It is a good point at which to remember the destination of our journey and Pope Francis reminds us again of the victory of Jesus over sin and death. He shows how "the Church points out to us the end of this journey of conversion, namely participation in the glory of Christ, which shines on the face of the obedient Servant, who died and rose for us."[12]

It is the glory of God for which we are made; our sharing in this glory is not just the endpoint of our Lenten pilgrimage, but the whole point and purpose of our lives. This is what we were made for, to share in the glory and joy of God himself. To help us understand this, Jesus revealed his glory, or at least, as much as humanity could bear, to the disciples Peter, James and John. This event comes near the end of Jesus's life on earth and frames it, together with the event of his Baptism. Both are Trinitarian in nature; the voice of the Father is heard referring to Jesus his Son and the Holy Spirit is present. At the Baptism of the Lord, the Holy Spirit is seen in the form of a dove, but here there is a cloud from which the Father speaks. This reminds us of the cloud that directed the Israelites on their way to the Promised Land (*Ex* 14:19); it is the glory of the divine presence.

The glory of God then, is not only an encouraging, or even frightening, sight for the disciples. It has the power to prepare them for the biggest test of their faith so far. We recall how in the first reading for this Sunday, Abraham's faith is tested to the point where he is able to offer even his only son to God in obedience. Now the Apostles will be asked for an even greater acceptance of God's plan for humanity – this time, Jesus, unlike Isaac, will actually enter into death.

In his perfect obedience to the Father, Jesus is the perfect icon of the Father and thus reveals his glory. The Holy Father tells us that:

"He is the fulfilment of revelation; that is why beside him appear transfigured, Moses and Elijah appear; they represent the Law and the Prophets, so as to signify that everything finishes and begins in Jesus, in his Passion and in his glory."[13]

The light that emanated from Jesus points to the glory of the Resurrection. The Holy Father has often reflected on the Transfiguration and how this helps us prepare for the cross, knowing how there will be another face of Jesus to look on between the glory of the Transfiguration and that of the Resurrection; the face of the cross.

"Between this beautiful transfiguration and that Resurrection there will be another face of Jesus. There will be a face that's not so beautiful."[14]

> You were transfigured on the mountain, and your disciples, as much as they were capable of it, beheld your glory, O Christ our God, so that when they should see you crucified they would understand that your Passion was voluntary, and proclaim to the world that you truly are the splendour of the Father.[15]

Pope Francis points out the link between this transfiguration and revelation of glory and the love which is the very nature of God.

"His full adherence to God's will renders his humanity transparent to the glory of God, who is love."[16]

The glory of this love is what we are promised, what we are here on earth to receive and give to others. Far from being a sentimental feeling, our love has to experience both the trials of the desert and the radiance of God's glory, but we are assured of true happiness if we endure.

> The path to Jesus always leads us to happiness, don't forget it! Jesus's way always leads us to happiness.

There will always be a cross, trials in the middle, but at the end we are always led to happiness. Jesus does not deceive us, he promised us happiness and will give it to us if we follow his ways.[17]

May our Blessed Lady sustain us as we prepare to come down from the mountain and resume our desert journey to the cross and beyond.

Challenge: Pray to be ready for the cross which follows the Transfiguration.

THIRD SUNDAY OF LENT

God our Father, in your infinite love and goodness you have shown us that prayer, fasting and almsgiving are remedies for sin. Accept the humble admission of our guilt, and when our conscience weighs us down let your unfailing mercy raise us up. Through our Lord Jesus Christ, your Son, who lives and reigns with you in the unity of the Holy Spirit, one God, for ever and ever. Amen.[18]

Today in the readings at Mass we are given three key passages on which to ponder. The Old Testament reading gives us again the Ten Commandments – the base-line for all moral teaching and its foundation. Our response to this, the Church indicates in the psalm, is not to find God's law oppressive or restricting, but a delight, life to the soul and wisdom to the heart.

> The law of the Lord is perfect,
> It revives the soul.
> The rule of the Lord is to be trusted,
> It gives wisdom to the simple.
> The precepts of the Lord are right,
> They gladden the heart.
> The command of the Lord is clear,
> It gives light to the eyes. (*Ps* 19:7-8)

Pope Francis reminds us that:

> ...the law of the People of God...is the law of love, love for God and love for neighbour according to the new commandment that the Lord left to us (cf. *Jn* 13:34). It is a love, however, that is not sterile sentimentality or something vague, but the acknowledgement of God as the one Lord of life and, at the same time, the acceptance of the other as my true brother, overcoming division, rivalry, misunderstanding, selfishness; these two things go together.[19]

With this in our minds, we now hear St Paul acknowledging that the crucifixion of Christ will be an obstacle to many. The Jews want miracles, he says, and the Greeks want wisdom, and here we are, offering them a crucified Christ. It is one thing to keep the commandments, which are clearly good and sensible rules for everyday life; it is quite another to accept the crucified Christ as the Saviour of humanity.

The Gospel shows us how Jesus is aware of this. He sees that the Jewish authorities have strayed from the understanding of the Temple as the House of God and a place of prayer. They have perhaps loved the letter of the Law more than its spirit of love. Jesus also knows that they will not understand that he must be crucified and rise again; neither miracles nor Greek wisdom will be able to explain this. Nor will they understand that his own resurrected body is to become the temple in which all humanity can come to God, delighting in his law. Pope Francis tells us that the risen Christ is the meeting place between God and all mankind.

> His humanity is the true temple where God is revealed, speaks, is encountered; and the true worshippers, the true worshippers of God are not only the guardians of the material temple, the keepers of power and of religious knowledge, [but] they are those who worship God "in spirit and truth". (*Jn* 4:23)[20]

This prophetic action of Jesus in the Temple points forward to his trial and crucifixion in which his words would be deliberately misinterpreted by the authorities, but he points us beyond this to his Resurrection and the true worship of God. Pope Francis reminds us that:

> Every Eucharist that we celebrate with faith makes us grow as a living temple of the Lord, thanks to the communion with his crucified and risen Body. Jesus recognises what is in each of us, and knows well our most ardent desires: that of being inhabited by him, only by him.[21]

The early Fathers of the Church interpreted this account as an allegory. They saw the Temple sanctuary symbolising our undisciplined souls which are filled, not with animals, but with disordered love of worldly and worthless things. In order to help us truly love the law of God and to worship him in spirit and in truth, Jesus must drive these things from their foremost position in our hearts. We are not able to do this alone; it is only through the strength of Jesus himself that we are able to give him first place in our hearts and acknowledge him as Lord. This is the law of the Lord which will bring us true joy.

Hear us Lord, and have mercy; for we have sinned against you.
Listen, Christ, to the prayers of those who cry to you.[22]

Challenge: Pray for the spiritual discernment to identify those things which take up the first place in the temple of your heart which should be reserved for Jesus.

Fourth Sunday of Lent

We invoke your mercy in humble prayer, O Lord, that you may cause us, your servants, corrected by penance and schooled by good works, to persevere sincerely in your commands and come safely to the paschal festivities. Through our Lord Jesus Christ, your Son, who lives and reigns with you in the unity of the Holy Spirit, one God, for ever and ever. Amen.[23]

Today the Church gives us a partial account of the history of the sins of God's people and the consequences to the life of the nation. While it can be harmful to spend too much time dwelling on the past and what went wrong, it is essential to look clearly and honestly at the facts in order to avoid making the same mistakes over and over again. If we cannot learn from history we will be doomed to repeat it.

We should pay attention then to this history of failure before we move on to more comforting passages. We notice that, firstly, it is the heads of the priesthood who failed in faithfulness to God, though the people are included also. We see that they had become conformed to the ways of those surrounding them and, significantly, that they had defiled the Temple of God, reminding us of the anger of Jesus at those who misused the Temple. However, as soon as we hear of the sin, we hear of a remedy for it; God sends 'messenger after messenger', but all are mocked and ignored. Eventually enemies burn down the Temple, destroy Jerusalem and deport the surviving people. The Exile in Babylon is to have a profound effect on the people and it will be seventy years before they are allowed by another king to return and rebuild the Temple.

Pope Francis points out the retelling of salvation history contained in the fourth Eucharistic prayer.

> "Even when he disobeyed you and lost your friendship you did not abandon him to the power of death", but with your mercy "helped all men to seek and find you". He came with his mercy… And when "the fullness of time" arrived, despite the fact that man had repeatedly broken the covenant, God, rather than abandoning him, formed a new bond with him, in the blood of Jesus – the bond of a new and everlasting covenant – a bond that nothing will ever break.[24]

Elsewhere he writes: "The whole of salvation history is the story of God looking for us: he offers us love and welcomes us with tenderness."[25]

With this in mind we can understand the meaning of that well known verse in the Gospel where Jesus is speaking with Nicodemus. "God loved the world so much that he gave his only Son, so that everyone who believes in him may not be lost but may have eternal life." (*Jn* 3:16)

The cross of Christ is the supreme proof of the mercy and love that God has for us: Jesus loved us "to the end" (*Jn* 13:1), meaning not only to the last instant of his earthly life, but to the farthest limit of love. While in creation the Father gave us proof of his immense love by giving us life, in the Passion and death of his Son he gave us the proof of proofs: he came to suffer and die for us. So great is God's mercy: he loves us, he forgives us; God forgives all and God forgives always.[26]

The seventeenth century poet John Donne understood this well. "One of the most convenient hieroglyphics of God is a circle and a circle is endless. Whom God loves, he loves to the end; and not only to their own end, to their death, but to his end, and his end is that he might love them still."[27]

St Paul, writing to the Ephesians, tells us that we are God's 'work of art', his 'design' (*Ep* 2:10). His love for us is so great that he has poured out grace upon us as a gift. None of us can claim credit for this, Paul says, we are saved by this grace and elevated by it to become God's children, destined to live with him in heaven. Pope Francis speaks of this great love:

This is the simplest expression that epitomises all of the Gospel, all of the faith, all of theology: God loves us with a free and boundless love... At the beginning of the world there is only the freely given love of the Father. St Irenaeus, a saint of the first centuries, writes:

"In the beginning, therefore, did God form Adam, not as if he stood in need of man, but that he might have one upon whom to confer his benefits" (*Adversus Haereses*, IV, 14, 1). It is like this, God's love is like this.[28]

Challenge: How will you respond to such a great love?

Fifth Sunday of Lent

*By your help, we beseech you, Lord our God, may
we walk eagerly in that same charity with which, out
of love for the world, your Son handed himself over
to death. Through our Lord Jesus Christ, your Son,
who lives and reigns with you in the unity of the Holy
Spirit, one God, for ever and ever.*[29]

Today the Old Testament reading takes up a theme which
is dear to the heart of Pope Francis and to which he often
returns. The new covenant which God will make with his
people is proclaimed by the prophet Jeremiah, who must
have been glad of some good news to proclaim. This is not
to be a covenant like the old one when Moses brought the
people out of Egypt and to which they could not remain
faithful. This new covenant is to be one of the heart. It will
be planted by God 'deep within' the people – 'written' on
their hearts. In fact, it will be so deeply implanted that there
will almost be no need to speak of it – everyone will be in
communion with God and with each other in this way.

Pope Francis highlights:

…the newness which characterises this people: it truly
involves a new people, which is based on the New
Covenant, established by the Lord Jesus with the gift

of his life. This newness does not deny the previous journey nor does it oppose it, but in fact leads it forth, leads it to fulfilment.[30]

This deep and internal communion with God is what the Holy Father so often exhorts us to embrace, and not just as individuals.

Returning to the Lord "with all your heart" means to begin the journey not of a superficial and transitory conversion, but rather of a spiritual itinerary with regard to the most intimate place of our person. The heart is, indeed, the seat of our feelings, the centre in which our decisions, our attitudes mature. That "return to me with all your heart" involves not only individuals, but is extended to the community as a whole.[31]

As we have seen, this conversion of heart, based as it is in the new Covenant of love which has the crucified Christ at its centre, is more difficult to accept for some people and cultures than for others. The Jewish leaders hoped for signs and miracles, had experienced them from God in the past, and indeed Jesus did perform them. The Greek culture which was still prevalent in that time and place, relied heavily upon human thought and reason, drawing on the wisdom of its great philosophers. Of course, neither of these would stand alone as St John Paul II knew so well.

Faith and reason are like two wings on which the human spirit rises to the contemplation of truth; and God has placed in the human heart a desire to know the truth – in a word, to know himself – so that, by knowing and loving God, men and women may also come to the fullness of truth about themselves.[32]

Whether Jew or Greek, people are drawn to Jesus in whose Person all human faith and reason are combined with his sacrificial love for humanity. And so it is in today's Gospel when 'some Greeks' are brought to our attention. We know almost nothing about them, but the two facts we are given are all we need to know before they vanish from the pages of Scripture again. Firstly, we know that they are attracted to the Jewish faith in some way as they had come up to Jerusalem to worship at the Passover feast. They may have been converts to the Jewish faith, or simply attracted to it, though 'worship' would imply some degree of engagement. Secondly, we know that they wanted to see Jesus. At this stage, Jesus has become very well known. He has recently raised Lazarus from the dead and has just entered Jerusalem to the palm waving and hosannas of a multitude of people. It is no wonder the Greeks were curious.

Pope Francis points out how this desire to see God is written upon the human heart; God has written this new covenant in Christ Jesus on our hearts also:

"We wish to see Jesus": these words, like so many others in the Gospels, go beyond this particular episode and express something universal; they reveal a desire that passes through the ages and cultures, a desire present in the heart of so many people who have heard of Christ, but have not yet encountered him.[33]

Perhaps Philip spoke good Greek; his own name is a Greek one. At any rate, he was able to organise a meeting with Jesus through Andrew, but we do not hear of any individual conversation Jesus may have had with the Greeks. We hear rather of his response to how this universal desire to see God – to see him – God the Son – will be fulfilled. Pope Francis explains:

"The hour has come for the Son of Man to be glorified" (*Jn* 12:23). It is the hour of the cross! It is the time for the defeat of Satan, prince of evil, and of the definitive triumph of the merciful love of God. Christ declares that he will be "lifted up from the earth" (v. 32), an expression with a twofold meaning: "lifted" because he is crucified, and "lifted" because he is exalted by the Father in the Resurrection, to draw everyone to him and to reconcile mankind with God and among themselves.[34]

Challenge: How would you respond if someone came to you wanting to meet Jesus?

Palm Sunday

Almighty ever-living God, who as an example of humility for the human race to follow caused our Saviour to take flesh and submit to the cross, graciously grant that we may heed his lesson of patient suffering and so merit a share in his Resurrection. Who lives and reigns with you in the unity of the Holy Spirit, one God, for ever and ever.[35]

Today, as we hear the words of St Paul, our attention is drawn to the humility of Jesus. Not only has he humbled himself to take on the human condition even though he is God the Son, second Person of the Most Holy Trinity, but he has humbled himself still further to accept a human death, and not an ordinary death but a shameful death by crucifixion. No wonder St Paul tells us in his letter to the Corinthians that "God's foolishness is wiser than human wisdom and God's weakness is stronger than human strength." (*1 Co* 1:25, Third Sunday of Lent)

Pope Francis takes up this theme:

Humility is above all God's way: God humbles himself to walk with his people, to put up with their infidelity… This is God's way, the way of humility. It is *the* way of Jesus; there is no other. And there can be no humility without humiliation. Following this path to the full, the Son of God took on the *"form of a slave"* (cf. *Ph* 2:7). In the end, humility means *service*. It means making room for God by *stripping* oneself, *"emptying* oneself", as Scripture says (v. 7). This is the greatest humiliation of all.[36]

Jesus came to Jerusalem in the full knowledge that he would be humiliated, that he would undergo suffering and death. Yet even as he allowed the crowd to welcome him as King and Messiah, he was humbling himself in fulfilling the prophecy of Zechariah.

"Lo, your king comes to you; triumphant and victorious is he, humble and riding on an ass, on a colt the foal of an ass." (*Zc* 9:9)

The coming of Jesus was accomplished right from the start in humility. The Annunciation was made to a humble Jewish girl and the birth of Jesus was in a temporary shelter in a stable. The childhood of our Lord is largely unknown to us, but took place in a humble carpenter's shop, not the palace of a king. And we see the same humility in his entrance to the place where he was to accomplish the saving of humanity.

"Jesus's entry into Jerusalem manifested the coming of the kingdom that the King-Messiah was going to accomplish by the Passover of his death and Resurrection. It is with the celebration of that entry on Palm Sunday that the Church's liturgy solemnly opens Holy Week." (*CCC* 560)

For ourselves, as we accompany Jesus by listening on Palm Sunday to the account of his Passion, we will do well to consider our own smallness and humility. The Holy Father reminds us that:

Humility is the virtue of the childlike and this is true humility and not a rather theatrical humility: no, not that: the humility of somebody who said: "I am humble but proud of being so." No, that is not true humility… The humility of the childlike is that of somebody who walks in the presence of the Lord, does not speak badly about others, looks only at serving and feels that he or she is the smallest.[37]

As we have journeyed through Lent, we will have battled with our own failings; perhaps we have not fasted as much as we intended, fallen into the trap of rushing through our prayers and given little in the way of alms. Perhaps though, we have done all these things to the best of our ability and are struggling with finding the necessary humility to offer them to God without expectation of public reward. But we should not feel despondent at our failures, but rather offer them – spread them before our Lord as the crowd spread their branches and cloaks. On that first Palm Sunday, the crowd had high hopes of what was to come – they didn't anticipate the death of the one they welcomed as Messiah. For ourselves also, even though our attempts to keep a good Lent may fall short of our expectations, we too can hold on to the hope that Jesus brings eternally. Pope Francis reminds us that:

> Jesus has awakened great hopes, especially in the hearts of the simple, the humble, the poor, the forgotten, those who do not matter in the eyes of the world. He understands human sufferings, he has shown the face of God's mercy, he has bent down to heal body and soul.[38]

"Hosanna, blessed is he who comes in the name of the Lord; blessed is the kingdom of our father David which is coming to us; Hosanna in heaven above." (*Mk* 11:9-10)

Challenge: Pray for the humility to discern our failings and to offer them to God.

HOLY WEEK AND TRIDUUM

MASS OF CHRISM

O God, who anointed your Only Begotten Son with the Holy Spirit and made him Christ and Lord, graciously grant that, being made sharers in his consecration, we may bear witness to your Redemption in the world. Through our Lord Jesus Christ, your Son, who lives and reigns with you in the unity of the Holy Spirit, one God, for ever and ever.[39]

Usually celebrated on Thursday of Holy Week (though sometimes earlier in the week), the Mass of Chrism focuses on the holy oils used by the Church in the sacraments to enable the faithful to encounter the risen Christ. Three oils are consecrated at this Mass. The Oil of Chrism is used in Baptism, Confirmation and Ordination – the sacraments which place the permanent seal of the Holy Spirit upon the soul. Perfumed with balsam, it is also used in the consecration of a Church and the dedicating of an altar. The Oil of the Sick is used in the Sacrament of the Sick and the Oil of Catechumens for those who are preparing for Baptism. After Mass the oils are taken away to be distributed among the parishes at the evening Mass of the Lord's Supper.

Pope Francis has meditated upon the psalm for the Chrism Mass, noting how it speaks of the love of God and his care for those who serve him in the priesthood.

"My hand shall ever abide with him, my arms also shall strengthen him" (*Ps* 89:21).

This is what the Lord means when he says: "I have found David, my servant; with my holy oil I have anointed him" (v. 20). It is also what our Father thinks whenever he "encounters" a priest. And he goes on to say: "My faithfulness and my steadfast love shall be with him... He shall cry to me, 'You are my Father, my God and the rock of my salvation'" (vv. 24, 26).[40]

The Lord knows the work of a priest is not easy, the Pope notes. Weariness is always present and Pope Francis is aware of the tiredness and fatigue experienced by good and faithful priests who have the care of souls at heart.

Do you know how often I think about this weariness which all of you experience? I think about it and I pray about it, often, especially when I am tired myself. I pray for you as you labour amid the people of God entrusted to your care, many of you in lonely and dangerous places. Our weariness, dear priests, is like incense which silently rises up to heaven (cf. *Ps* 141:2; *Rv* 8:3-4). Our weariness goes straight to the heart of the Father.[41]

The priest is called to share in the threefold office of Christ, who is anointed Prophet, Priest and King, in a certain way, but all of us are called to share in the threefold office in a manner most suited to our own state of life.

"Jesus Christ is the one whom the Father anointed with the Holy Spirit and established as Priest, Prophet, and King. The whole People of God participates in these three offices of Christ and bears the responsibilities for mission and service that flow from them." (*CCC* 783)

> The participation of the lay faithful in the threefold mission of Christ as Priest, Prophet and King finds its source in the anointing of Baptism, its further development in Confirmation and its realisation and dynamic sustenance in the Holy Eucharist. It is a participation given to each member of the lay faithful individually, in as much as each is one of the many who form the one Body of the Lord.[42]

This means that each one of us will share in the weariness of the priest, each of us will be weighed down with the burden of work for the Kingdom, and the Holy Father points out that the weariness of each one is known to God and to his Blessed Mother who knows when her children are tired.

The Holy Father tells us that:

> Our weariness is precious in the eyes of Jesus who embraces us and lifts us up. "Come to me, all who labour

and are overburdened, and I will give you rest" (*Mt* 11:28). Whenever a priest feels dead tired, yet is able to bow down in adoration and say: "Enough for today Lord", and entrust himself to the Father, he knows that he will not fall but be renewed. The one who anoints God's faithful people with oil is also himself anointed by the Lord: "He gives you a garland instead of ashes, the oil of gladness instead of mourning, the mantle of praise instead of a faint spirit" (cf. *Is* 61:3).[43]

Praise to you, O Christ, king of eternal glory!
The spirit of the Lord has been given to me.
He has sent me to bring the good news to the poor.
Praise to you, O Christ, king of eternal glory![44]

Challenge: Pray for your priest before you go to sleep tonight.

HOLY THURSDAY,
MASS OF THE LORD'S SUPPER

Grant us, O Lord, we pray, that we may participate worthily in these mysteries, for whenever the memorial of this sacrifice is celebrated the work of our redemption is accomplished. Through Christ our Lord. Amen.[45]

Pope Francis returns to one of his favourite themes at this Mass; the endless love of God for us.

"Now before the feast of the Passover, when Jesus knew that his hour had come to depart out of this world to the Father, having loved his own who were in the world, he loved them to the end." (*Jn* 13:1)

We hear the Gospel for this Mass in a slightly different translation, but the translation chosen by the Holy Father for his remarks emphasises the endless love of Christ for 'his own'.[46] The Pope cannot emphasise this enough:

Jesus's love for us knows no limits: always more and more. He never tires of loving anyone. He loves us all, to the point of giving his life for us. Yes, giving his life for us; yes, giving his life for all of us, giving his life for each one of us. And every one of us can say: "He gave his life for me". …He never tires of loving, just as he never tires of forgiving, never tires of embracing us. This is the first thing that I wanted to say to you: Jesus loved us, every one of us, to the end.[47]

This love, the love of Jesus for those who belong to him, is what gives his sacrifice on the cross its redemptive value.

This great love remains with us in a special way through the Sacrament of the Eucharist, in which Christ's redemptive Sacrifice is truly present in our midst. We also experience his unlimited love and mercy in the Sacrament of Reconciliation. His death on the cross incarnates perfectly the new commandment he gave to his disciples.[48]

We see again in the action of Jesus in washing his disciples' feet the humility of which St Paul wrote. Jesus Christ, God the Son who with the Father and the Holy Spirit created the world and holds everything in being, has not only entered the world but has chosen to live in it as a slave, the lowest human condition. The Holy Father notes that, at this time, it was usual for those who had travelled to arrive with their feet dusty from the roads.

…at the entrance to the house, they washed their feet. It was not done by the master of the house but by the slaves. That was the task of a slave. And like a slave, Jesus washes our feet, the feet of his disciples, and that is why he says: "What I am doing you do not know now, but afterward you will understand" (*Jn* 13:7). Jesus's love is so great that he became a slave to serve us, to heal us, to cleanse us.[49]

Peter, who with the other disciples, is often slow to grasp what Jesus is truly doing and saying, is horrified to see Jesus prepare to perform the task of a slave. After all, he has seen this man cure the sick and raise the dead, feed the hungry from a small amount of food, walk on water, still the storm and turn water into wine. He can't bear to think of this happening and refuses to be part of it. But Jesus insists, emphasising he is indeed 'Lord and Master' and that it is exactly in this manner that the disciples should do as he does now. When we see our priests at this Mass – those men we hold in high regard in daily life – kneeling humbly on the hard floor, their hair disordered from the removal of garments – washing the feet of their parishioners, let us remember that we too are called to serve humbly and not hold fast to our worldly status in doing so.

However, this action of Jesus as a slave does not stand alone; it is the expression of that endless love which will continue through the night into the Gethsemane and Calvary. It merges seamlessly with the commandments of Jesus to "love one another as I have loved you" (*Jn* 13:34) and to continue to offer the Eucharistic sacrifice as a memorial of him (*Lk* 22:19, *1 Co* 11:24).

Pope Francis is clear in his teaching that the Eucharist:

...is not a private prayer or a beautiful spiritual experience, it's not simply a commemoration of what Jesus did in the Last Supper...(but) a memorial, namely, a gesture that actualises and makes present the event of the death and Resurrection of Jesus: the bread is truly his Body given, the wine is truly is Blood poured out.

To live in concrete communion with Jesus through the Eucharist while on earth is already the beginning of our passing from death to life...we close our eyes to this world in the certainty that on the last day we will hear the voice of Jesus Risen who will call us, and we will awaken to always be with him and with the great family of saints.[50]

Challenge: Give some time to prayer before the Blessed Sacrament at the Altar of Repose.

GOOD FRIDAY, THE LORD'S PASSION

Remember your mercies, O Lord, and with your eternal protection sanctify your servants, for whom Christ your Son, by the shedding of his Blood, established the Paschal Mystery. Who lives and reigns with you in the unity of the Holy Spirit, God for ever and ever.[51]

There is no Mass on Good Friday as the Church watches and prays, recalling the death of the Lord Jesus on the cross. There are four main parts to the liturgy today. Firstly, we hear from Scripture, especially a Gospel account of the Passion. Secondly, we pray for the whole world, beginning with the Church and widening the circle with every prayer to include all people, even those who do not acknowledge God at all. Next we venerate the cross, expressing our love and devotion to Jesus, and finally we receive Holy Communion which has been reserved for this time. During the Veneration of the Cross, the 'Reproaches' are often sung in some form and it is to some of these that we turn now.

The reproaches are written in the form of questions which Jesus might have asked of his people as he hung dying on the cross.

O my people, what have I done to you? How have I offended you? Answer me!

I led you out of Egypt, from slavery to freedom, but you led your Saviour to the cross.

For forty years I led you safely through the desert. I fed you with manna from heaven, and brought you to a land of plenty; but you led your Saviour to the cross.

What more could I have done for you? I planted you as my fairest vine, but you yielded only bitterness: when I was thirsty you gave me vinegar to drink, and you pierced your Saviour's side with a lance.

I opened the sea before you, but you opened my side with a spear.

I led you on your way in a pillar of cloud, but you led me to Pilate's court.

I bore you up with manna in the desert, but you struck me down and scourged me.

I gave you saving water from the rock, but you gave me gall and vinegar to drink.

I gave you a royal sceptre, but you gave me a crown of thorns.

I raised you to the height of majesty, but you have raised me high on a cross.

O my people, what have I done to you? How have I offended you? Answer me!

These questions are a way for us to reflect upon the injustices Jesus suffered in his death. All that he has done for us is good, yet we have treated him as though he were an enemy. Despite this, Father Raniero Cantalamessa, preacher of the Pontifical Household, reminds us that:

> Jesus died, crying out, "Father, forgive them; for they know not what they do" (*Lk* 23:34). This prayer was not simply murmured under his breath; it was cried out so that people could hear it as well. Neither is it even a prayer; it is a peremptory request made with the authority that comes from being the Son: "Father, forgive them!" And since he himself had said that the Father heard all his prayers (see *Jn* 11:42), we have to believe that he heard this last prayer from the cross and consequently that the crucifiers of Christ were then forgiven by God (not of course without in some way being repentant) and are with him in paradise, to testify for all eternity to what extremes the love of God is capable of going.[52]

As we venerate the cross this year, we might reflect upon the endless love of God the Son who, in loving obedience to the Father, won for us so great a redemption.

> It is love "to the end" that confers on Christ's sacrifice its value as redemption and reparation, as atonement and satisfaction. He knew and loved us all when he

offered his life. ...No man, not even the holiest, was ever able to take on himself the sins of all men and offer himself as a sacrifice for all. The existence in Christ of the divine person of the Son, who at once surpasses and embraces all human persons, and constitutes himself as the Head of all mankind, makes possible his redemptive sacrifice for all. (*CCC* 616)

Whom God loves, he loves to the end.

Challenge: Place a crucifix in a prominent position in your home if this is possible. If not, carry a small crucifix with you today and touch it frequently.

Holy Saturday, the Paschal Vigil

O God, who by the light of the New Testament have unlocked the meaning of wonders worked in former times, so that the Red Sea prefigures the sacred font and the nation delivered from slavery foreshadows the Christian people, grant, we pray, that all nations, obtaining the privilege of Israel by merit of faith, may be reborn by partaking of your Spirit. Through Christ our Lord. Amen.[53]

By most ancient tradition, this is the night of keeping vigil for the Lord (*Ex* 12:42), in which, following the Gospel admonition (*Lk* 12:35-37), the faithful, carrying lighted lamps in their hands, should be like those looking for the Lord when he returns, so that at his coming he may find them awake and have them sit at his table.

On this most sacred night, in which our Lord Jesus Christ passed over from death to life, the Church calls upon her sons and daughters, scattered throughout the world, to come together to watch and pray. If we keep the memorial of the Lord's paschal solemnity in this way, listening to his word and celebrating his mysteries, then we shall have the sure hope of sharing his triumph over death and living with him in God.[54]

As we keep this vigil, we recall how the disciples also kept vigil on that night before the Resurrection. Pope Francis observes that "This was a night of vigil for the disciples of Jesus, a night of sadness and fear. The men remained locked in the Upper Room." But God is not sleeping.

> ...the Watchman is watching over his people (cf. *Ps* 121:4), to bring them out of slavery and to open before them the way to freedom. The Lord is keeping watch and, by the power of his love, he is bringing his people through the Red Sea. He is also bringing Jesus through the abyss of death and the netherworld.[55]

The Holy Father points out that the women also kept watch that night. They were waiting for the dawn in a way they did not yet understand and they were waiting to enter into the tomb, even though they did not see how this could be done. However, they did not remain "prisoners of fear and sadness"; they went to the tomb anyway, in spite of their grief and anxiety.

> They went forth and found the tomb open. And they went in. They had kept watch, they went forth and they entered into the Mystery. May we learn from them to keep watch with God and with Mary our Mother, so that we too may enter into the Mystery which leads from death to life.[56]

Pope Francis tells us that we too must enter into the mystery of the tomb.

> "To enter into the mystery" means the ability to wonder, to contemplate; the ability to listen to the silence and to hear the tiny whisper amid great silence by which God speaks to us… To enter the mystery demands that we not be afraid of reality… To enter into the mystery means…going out in search of truth, beauty and love…seeking a deeper meaning… To enter into the mystery, we need humility…we need to adore. Without adoration, we cannot enter into the mystery.[57]

These words tie together the thoughts that the Holy Father has shared with us during Lent. We need the humility to ponder on the mysteries of our faith whilst understanding that we shall not 'solve' those mysteries as though they were a puzzle. Our hearts must become that quiet place, like the tomb, where we ponder on those mysteries and enter into them ever more deeply. Like Mary, may we keep all these things in our hearts. (*Lk* 2:51)

At the start of the Easter Vigil we will have heard at least part of the *Exultet*, that wonderful hymn to God which proclaims his great works for us, starting with creation and the fall of Adam, recalling the night of the Passover and exodus from Egypt, with the pillars of cloud and fire to guide, and linking all with the light of Christ's Resurrection from the dead. Pope Francis reminds us elsewhere that:

There is an urgent need…to see once again that faith is a light, for once the flame of faith dies out, all other lights begin to dim. The light of faith is unique, since it is capable of illuminating every aspect of human existence. A light this powerful cannot come from ourselves but from a more primordial source: in a word, it must come from God. Faith is born of an encounter with the living God who calls us and reveals his love, a love which precedes us and upon which we can lean for security and for building our lives.[58]

Therefore, O Lord, we pray you that this candle, hallowed to the honour of your name, may persevere undimmed, to overcome the darkness of this night. Receive it as a pleasing fragrance, and let it mingle with the lights of heaven. May this flame be found still burning by the Morning Star: the one Morning Star who never sets, Christ your Son, who, coming back from death's domain, has shed his peaceful light on humanity, and lives and reigns for ever and ever. Amen.[59]

Challenge: Light a candle and pray for the souls of all those you know who have died, naming as many as you can recall.

EASTERTIDE

Easter Sunday

O God, who on this day through your Only Begotten Son, have conquered death and unlocked for us the path to eternity, grant, we pray, that we who keep the solemnity of the Lord's Resurrection may, through the renewal brought by your Spirit, rise up in the light of life. Through our Lord Jesus Christ, your Son, who lives and reigns with you in the unity of the Holy Spirit, one God, for ever and ever. Amen.[60]

Alleluia! Christ is risen! He is risen indeed! Alleluia!

With these words we welcome with Pope Francis the hope fulfilled on Easter Morning, as does the whole Christian world.

Love has triumphed over hatred, life has conquered death, light has dispelled the darkness!

Out of love for us, Jesus Christ stripped himself of his divine glory, emptied himself, took on the form of a slave and humbled himself even to death, death on a cross. For this reason God exalted him and made him Lord of the universe. Jesus is Lord![61]

Even in the midst of this rejoicing, the Holy Father recalls the theme that has been so close to his heart throughout

Lent; the humility of the Lord and his willingness to take on, not only our humanity, but the lowest position of a slave who is counted as nothing by the world.

> By his death and Resurrection, Jesus shows everyone the way to life and happiness: this way is humility, which involves humiliation. This is the path which leads to glory. Only those who humble themselves can go towards the "things that are above", towards God (cf. *Col* 3:1-4). The proud look "down from above"; the humble look "up from below".

> On Easter morning, alerted by the women, Peter and John ran to the tomb. They found it open and empty. Then they drew near and "bent down" in order to enter it. To enter into the mystery, we need to "bend down", to abase ourselves. Only those who abase themselves understand the glorification of Jesus and are able to follow him on his way.[62]

For Peter and John on that first Easter morning, that 'bending low' to enter the tomb resulted in their receiving the first sign of the Resurrection. An empty tomb is not, as the *Catechism of the Catholic Church* points out, direct evidence of the Resurrection itself, as it could be explained in other ways, but it is an essential first sign. (Cf. *CCC* 640)

Corresponding with our need to 'bend low' is the need for us to have the humility to accept that we cannot know the time, nor the manner of Christ's Resurrection. "No one was an eyewitness to Christ's Resurrection and no evangelist describes it. No one can say how it came about physically. Still less was its innermost essence, his passing over to another life, perceptible to the senses." (*CCC* 647) We can only accept and believe the testimony of others in humility and childlike trust.

"Although the Resurrection was an historical event that could be verified by the sign of the empty tomb and by the reality of the Apostles' encounters with the risen Christ, still it remains at the very heart of the mystery of faith as something that transcends and surpasses history." (*CCC* 647)

The Resurrection is the centre of our faith, a living light which has shone for two thousand years to light the way. This Easter Sunday we rejoice as children of God, in that same light.

At Easter, on the morning of the first day of the week, God said once again: "Let there be light". The night on the Mount of Olives, the solar eclipse of Jesus's Passion and death, the night of the grave had all passed. Now it is the first day once again – creation is beginning anew. "Let there be light", says God, "and there was light": Jesus rises from the grave. Life is stronger than death. Good is stronger than evil. Love is stronger than hate. Truth is stronger than lies. The darkness of the previous days is driven away the moment Jesus rises from the grave and himself becomes God's pure light. But this applies not only to him, not only to the darkness of those days. With the Resurrection of Jesus, light itself is created anew. He draws all of us after him into the new light of the Resurrection and he conquers all darkness. He is God's new day, new for all of us.[63]

Alleluia! He is risen indeed.

Challenge: Light a candle in your home and be ready to explain what Easter means.

Second Sunday of Easter

God of eternal compassion, each Easter you rekindle the faith of your consecrated people. Give them still greater grace, so that all may truly understand the waters in which they were cleansed, the Spirit by which they were reborn, the blood by which they were redeemed. Through our Lord Jesus Christ, your Son, who lives and reigns with you in the unity of the Holy Spirit, one God, for ever and ever. Amen.[64]

This Sunday marks the eighth day of Easter; the Easter Octave. This feast is so central to our Christian faith that one day to celebrate it is not enough; we have a whole week of Easters which we have just celebrated. And even after that, Eastertide continues on until Pentecost, fifty days after the Resurrection such is its significance for the world.

As St Paul tells us, "If Christ has not been raised, then our preaching is in vain and your faith is in vain." (*1 Co* 15:14)

Christ's Resurrection is the fulfilment of the promises both of the Old Testament and of Jesus himself during his earthly life... The truth of Jesus's divinity is confirmed by his Resurrection. He had said: "When you have lifted up the Son of man, then you will know that I am he." The Resurrection of the crucified one shows that he was truly "I AM", the Son of God and God himself. So St Paul could declare to the Jews: "What God promised to the fathers, this he has fulfilled to us their children by raising Jesus." (*CCC* 652-3)

All the promises made to God's people in the Old Testament are now fulfilled for us to share.

The Church shares the joy of Mary in the Resurrection of her Son and during the Easter season sings the *Regina Caeli* to her, knowing she never doubted the promises of God. Pope Francis points out that "The Lord proclaimed 'blessed', those who believe without seeing (cf. v. 29) the first of which is Mary his Mother."[65]

Regina Caeli, laetare, alleluia.	Queen of Heaven, rejoice, alleluia.
Quia quem meruisti portare, alleluia.	For he whom you did merit to bear, alleluia.
Resurrexit, sicut dixit, alleluia.	Has risen, as he said, alleluia.
Ora pro nobis Deum, alleluia.	Pray for us to God, alleluia.

But everyone does not have the strong faith and abundant grace which Mary received from God so willingly. Thomas, one of the Twelve who had been with Jesus for so long, one who had even seen him raise the dead, for some reason could not accept that Jesus himself was truly risen. Perhaps he dared not believe; it must have seemed too good to be true. He certainly seems to have taken a rather gloomy outlook on life as we see when Jesus went to Bethany after the death of Lazarus. "Thomas, called the Twin, said to his fellow disciples, 'Let us also go, that we may die with him.'" (*Jn* 11:16)

Whatever Thomas's reasons for doubt, our Lord did not leave him lost in his disbelief. Thomas, Pope Francis suggests, wasn't satisfied and wanted his own personal experience. Jesus, who knew Thomas so well, as he knows all of us, treated him with loving patience so that Thomas could take up the mission of the Gospel.

> Jesus waited for him patiently and offered himself to the difficulties and uncertainty of the last to arrive. … He also met the needs of the doubting disciple: "Put your finger here, and see my hands..." (v. 27). In the redeeming contact with the wounds of the Risen One, Thomas showed his own wounds, his own injuries, his own lacerations, his own humiliation; in the print of the nails he found the decisive proof that he was loved, that he was expected, that he was understood. He found himself before the Messiah filled with kindness, mercy, tenderness.[66]

Many years ago, another Pope, St Gregory the Great, pondered in a homily on the mystery of Doubting Thomas.

Dearly beloved, what do you see in these events? Do you really believe that it was by chance that this chosen disciple was absent, then came and heard, heard and doubted, doubted and touched, touched and believed? It was not by chance but in God's providence. In a marvellous way God's mercy arranged that the disbelieving disciple, in touching the wounds of his master's body, should heal our wounds of disbelief. *The disbelief of Thomas has done more for our faith than the faith of the other disciples*. As he touches Christ and is won over to belief, every doubt is cast aside and our faith is strengthened. So the disciple who doubted, then felt Christ's wounds, becomes a witness to the reality of the Resurrection.[67]

Pope Francis points out that, "on this Second Sunday of Easter we are called to contemplate, in the wounds of the Risen One, Divine Mercy, which overcomes all human limitations and shines on the darkness of evil and of sin."

Challenge: Consider how we can show mercy to others without compromising the truth of our faith.

THIRD SUNDAY OF EASTER

Christ, you are the light of the world and the salvation of nations; set us on fire with your Spirit as we proclaim the wonder of your Resurrection. Let Israel recognise in you the Messiah it has longed for; fill all men with the knowledge of your glory. Keep us united in the communion of saints; may we find rest with them, when life's work is done. You have overcome death, the last enemy of man; destroy everything in us that is at enmity with God.[68]

Pope Francis observes that twice in the readings at Mass we hear the term 'witness'.

> The first time it is on the lips of Peter who, after the healing of the paralytic at the Door of the Temple of Jerusalem, exclaims: You "killed the Author of life, whom God raised from the dead. To this we are witnesses" (*Ac* 3:15). The second time it is on the lips of the Risen Jesus. On the evening of Easter he opens the minds of the disciples to the mystery of his death and Resurrection, saying to them: "You are witnesses to these things" (*Lk* 24:48).[69]

The Apostles, the Pope notes, could not keep silent about what they had seen and heard. They could not help but be witnesses to such an extraordinary event; they had seen these things with their own eyes.

The word 'witness' is, in Greek, μάρτυς, or 'martyrs' and has two strands to its meaning today. Firstly, it means to be a direct observer of an event or fact so as to testify to the truth of its happening. Secondly, it means to grasp the truth of something which has not been directly observed, but has been reached by reasoning or faith.[70] However, in New Testament times, the witness was simply committed to proclaiming the truth, whether of fact or faith, and in these passages we see both aspects. The Apostles have seen the facts of the events, and they have grasped the profound truth of their meaning, for which they are ready to give their lives as martyrs. As Pope Francis remarks, "A witness is a person who has seen with an objective eye, has seen reality, but not with an indifferent eye; he has seen and has let himself become involved in the event." We too, though not eye-witnesses, are called to testify to the truth of the Resurrection. Jesus showed himself to his Apostles:

> so that the truth of his Resurrection would reach everyone by way of their witness. The Church has the duty to continue this mission over time. Every baptised person is called to bear witness, with their life

and words, that Jesus is Risen, that Jesus is alive and present among us. We are all called to testify that Jesus is alive.[71]

The Holy Father urges us to remember that when we think of what is involved in Christian 'witness', we do not mean "an ideology or a complex system of precepts and prohibitions or a moralist theory". This is not an abstract idea, but a person, the Person of Jesus Christ, God the Son who comes to us with the message of salvation, the Risen Lord and Saviour.

> He can be testified to by those who have personal experience of him, in prayer and in the Church, through a journey that has its foundation in Baptism, its nourishment in the Eucharist, its seal in Confirmation, its continual conversion in Penitence. Thanks to this journey, ever guided by the Word of God, every Christian can become a witness of the Risen Jesus.[72]

However, we should not forget that martyrdom is the supreme witness to the truth of Christ. In becoming witnesses we open ourselves not only to disbelief and scorn, but also to persecution and danger. This may not be the cruel tortures of earlier times, at least not yet in the United Kingdom, but the witnessing of faith in the current social climate has already led to jobs lost and court cases suffered. The Church is clear on what we should expect:

The disciple of Christ must not only keep the faith and live on it, but also profess it, confidently bear witness to it, and spread it: "All however must be prepared to confess Christ before men and to follow him along the way of the cross, amidst the persecutions which the Church never lacks." Service of and witness to the faith are necessary for salvation: "So every one who acknowledges me before men, I also will acknowledge before my Father who is in heaven; but whoever denies me before men, I also will deny before my Father who is in heaven." (*CCC* 1816)

We are called to bear witness to the truth. Jesus himself is the truth; he is the Way, the Truth and the Life, and he is the only way to the Father. (*Jn* 14:6)

"May Mary our Mother sustain us by her intercession, that we might become, with all our limitations but by the grace of faith, witnesses of the Risen Lord, bringing the Paschal gifts of joy and peace to the people we encounter."[73]

Challenge: Today wear some small outward sign of your Christian faith.

FOURTH SUNDAY OF EASTER

Almighty ever-living God, lead us to a share in the joys of heaven, so that the humble flock may reach where the brave shepherd has gone before. Who lives and reigns with you in the unity of the Holy Spirit, one God for ever and ever. Amen.[74]

This Sunday is known also as 'Good Shepherd' Sunday because each year we hear the reading from St John's Gospel, chapter 10, where Jesus tells us he is the Good Shepherd, a shepherd who not only cares for his flock and 'leads them beside still waters', but one who is willing to 'lay down his life' for his flock. We are so used to hearing this that perhaps it no longer strikes us as extraordinary that a shepherd would be prepared to die to defend his flock. Take some risk, maybe, to rescue one or two, or to fight off the wolves, as David did (*1 S* 17:34-37), but to actually die for them? This is an amazing insight into the love of Christ for those who are his.

"The good shepherd lays down his life for the sheep" (*Jn* 10:11): these words are wholly fulfilled when Christ, freely obeying the will of the Father, is immolated on the cross. The significance that he is "the Good Shepherd" thus becomes completely clear: he gives life, he offered his life in sacrifice for us all: for you, for me, for everyone![75]

This model of the Shepherd, willing to die for his sheep, is one on which the Holy Father invites us to contemplate. This shepherd gives his life freely; he is not forced to die, but lays down his life for the sheep.

Christ is the true shepherd, who fulfils the loftiest model of love for the flock: He freely lays down his own life, no one takes it from him (cf. v. 18), but he gives it for the sheep (v. 17). In open opposition to false shepherds, Jesus presents himself as the one true shepherd of the people.[76]

However, as Pope Francis points out in the same homily, "…it is not enough to contemplate and give thanks. It is also necessary to *follow* the Good Shepherd."

In the Western world we are not used to seeing sheep following a shepherd. It is far more usual for us to see sheep being driven, often by a well-trained sheepdog, *in front* of the shepherd rather than following behind him. In the time and place of Jesus, it was, and perhaps still is, more usual to see the shepherd walking in front of the sheep, looking out for danger and leading them to the places with the best grass and the least likelihood of steep cliff faces where they might fall. The flocks were smaller than we are accustomed to seeing and each sheep would be within hearing of the shepherd's voice which they knew well. The flock would only follow the voice they knew and trusted.

So what does it mean for us to follow Jesus, the Good Shepherd which Pope Francis tells us is necessary? How can we hear his voice? Pope St Gregory the Great challenged those to whom he preached to ask themselves:

> …whether you belong to his flock, whether you know him, whether the light of his truth shines in your minds. I assure you that it is not by faith that you will come to know him, but by love; not by mere conviction, but by action. John the Evangelist is my authority for this statement. He tells us that anyone who claims to know God without keeping his commandments is a liar.[77]

St John the Evangelist is indeed very clear on this. His writings, which speak so eloquently about the love of God for us and how we are to respond with love, nevertheless do not prevaricate. Indeed they echo the two great commandments with which our Lord summed up the Law; to love God and to love our neighbour.

"He who says 'I know him' but disobeys his commandments is a liar, and the truth is not in him; but whoever keeps his word, in him truly love for God is perfected. By this we may be sure that we are in him." (*1 Jn* 2:4-5)

"...we know that we love the children of God, when we love God and obey his commandments. For this is the love of God, that we keep his commandments. (*1 Jn* 5:2-3)

"And this is his commandment, that we should believe in the name of his Son Jesus Christ and love one another, just as he has commanded us." (*1 Jn* 3:23)

Good Shepherd Sunday is a day on which we particularly pray for vocations to the priesthood. We ask that God will send us good shepherds who will teach us to keep the commandments and shepherd the whole flock safely to the joys of heaven.

Pope Francis prays: "May Mary Most Holy obtain for me, for the bishops and for the priests of the entire world, the grace to serve the holy People of God through joyous preaching of the Gospel, heartfelt celebration of the sacraments, and patient and gentle pastoral guidance."[78]

Challenge: Pray for vocations to the priesthood today.

Fifth Sunday of Easter

Almighty ever-living God, constantly accomplish the Paschal Mystery within us, that those you were pleased to make new in Holy Baptism may, under your protective care, bear much fruit and come to the joys of life eternal. Through our Lord Jesus Christ, your Son, who lives and reigns with you in the unity of the Holy Spirit, one God, for ever and ever. Amen.[79]

We find in the readings today a strong theme of unity with Christ. This encompasses coming into unity with him as St Paul did after his conversion on the road to Damascus, not without difficulty as the disciples naturally did not trust him at first. It reiterates what we heard last week from St John, that if we love God we will keep his commandments to believe in Jesus the Son and to love one another, thus living in God and God living in us. And we hear the imagery of the vine which Jesus uses to illustrate the necessity of remaining in him, joined to him, in order to bear fruit.

Pope Francis takes up this theme of union with Christ, pointing out that the setting for this teaching is, significantly, the Last Supper and that, although the disciples may not have Jesus present with them in the way to which they have become accustomed, nevertheless he will remain present with them and will be united to them in a new way.

> For it is the last time he is with his disciples, and now he wants to impress firmly a fundamental truth in their minds: even when he will no longer be physically present in the midst of them, they will still be able to remain united to him in a new way, and thus bear much fruit. Everyone can be united to Jesus in a new way. If, on the contrary, one should lose this unity with him, this union with him, would become sterile, or rather, harmful to the community.[80]

What is this "new way" of which Jesus speaks? How are we to understand this way of being united to Jesus? We know that Jesus, the second Person of the Holy Trinity, was "by the Holy Spirit incarnate of the Virgin Mary and became man", so we know that our human nature is already joined, through the grace of God, to the divine nature. Pope Francis explains: "Jesus is the vine, and through him – like the sap in the tree – the very love of God, the Holy Spirit is passed to the branches."[81]

It is through the Holy Spirit that we are to be united to Christ, that same Spirit who moved on the face of the waters at Creation, inspired the prophets, 'overshadowed' Mary at the Annunciation and filled Elizabeth at the Visitation.

The Holy Father is clear on the way we are to be united to Jesus through the actions of the Holy Spirit. It is the sacraments which Jesus instituted that enable our union and intimacy with him and which are conferred in the power of the Holy Spirit.

> …we are the branches, and through this parable, Jesus wants us to understand the importance of remaining united to him. The branches are not self-sufficient, but depend totally on the vine, in which the source of their life is found. So it is with us Christians. Grafted by Baptism in Christ, we have freely received the gift of new life from him; and thanks to the Church we are able to remain in vital communion with Christ. We must remain faithful to Baptism, and grow in intimacy with the Lord through prayer, listening and docility to his Word – read the Gospel –, participation in the sacraments, especially the Eucharist and Reconciliation.[82]

Notice that the Pope includes prayer and listening to the Word of God with the sacraments; the sacraments do not stand alone as though they were some kind of magic action, but must be incorporated into a life lived in union with Christ through the Holy Spirit in every way. In fact, if we are living in union with Christ, we should be recognised by the fruits of such a life, just as one would recognise an apple tree by the fact that it is bearing apples. Everything bears fruit according to its nature, and if our nature is truly transformed though the Incarnation, the cross and Resurrection and our being joined to this through the sacraments, then our lives cannot help but bear the fruit of this, as Pope Francis remarks.

> When one is intimately united to Jesus, he enjoys the gifts of the Holy Spirit, which are – as St Paul tells us – "love, joy, peace, patience, kindness, generosity, faithfulness, gentleness, self-control" (*Ga* 5:22). These are the gifts that we receive if we remain united in Jesus; …The fruits of this profound union with Christ are wonderful: our whole person is transformed by the grace of the Spirit: soul, understanding, will, affections, and even body, because we are united body and soul.[83]

Come, Holy Spirit, fill the hearts of your faithful and kindle in them the fire of your love.

Challenge: Consider what would identify you as a Christian to a stranger who is getting to know you?

Sixth Sunday of Easter

*Almighty ever-living God, who restore us to eternal
life in the Resurrection of Christ, increase in us, we
pray, the fruits of this paschal Sacrament and pour
into our hearts the strength of this saving food.
Through Christ our Lord, Amen.*[84]

This Sunday Pope Francis has developed his previous
exploration of the connection between the sacraments,
especially the Eucharist, and the commandments of love.
Jesus says:

> "This is my commandment, that you love one another
> as I have loved you" (v. 12). Thinking of his imminent
> sacrifice on the cross, he adds: "Greater love has no man
> than this, that a man lay down his life for his friends.
> You are my friends, if you do what I command you" (v.
> 13-14). These words, said at the Last Supper, summarise
> Jesus's full message. Actually they summarise all that he
> did: Jesus gave his life for his friends. Friends who did
> not understand him, in fact they abandoned, betrayed
> and denied him at the crucial moment.[85]

The commandments of Jesus, so often summarised for the
disciples into a single commandment to love God and to
love one another, are seen to be inextricably linked to the

cross. These words of Jesus are spoken at the Last Supper where he instituted the Eucharist and commanded his disciples to continue to bring his sacrifice on the cross to his friends for all time in this way. So we have a threefold link; the commandments of Jesus, his death on the cross (in fact, the whole Paschal Mystery) and the Eucharist. "A threefold cord is not quickly broken", the writer of Ecclesiastes said in centuries past (*Qo* 4:12) and the Holy Father highlights this connection for us:

> This is the love that Jesus taught us. It is a new love because Jesus and his Spirit renewed it. It is a redeeming love, free from selfishness. A love which gives our hearts joy, as Jesus himself said: "These things I have spoken to you, that my joy may be in you, and that your joy may be full" (*Jn* 15:11).

> It is precisely Christ's love that the Holy Spirit pours into our hearts to make everyday wonders in the Church and in the world. There are many small and great actions which obey the Lord's commandment: "Love one another as I have loved you" (cf. *Jn* 15:12).[86]

And we are *enabled* to carry out those actions, to keep the commandments of love, through the grace of Christ poured into our heats at Baptism, strengthened at Confirmation and renewed and nourished by Reconciliation and the Eucharist as well as through the graces we receive through our own state of life.

We hear the prayers of Jesus for us in the Gospel today:

Holy Father, keep those you have given me true to your name, so that they may be one like us. While I was with them, I kept those you had given me true to your name. I have watched over them and not one is lost... Consecrate them in the truth. (*Jn* 17:11-12, 17)

Since Christ died and rose again, we are no longer confined to the possibilities of what we could achieve alone. We are new creatures now, empowered by the Holy Spirit through the sacraments which are rooted in the death and Resurrection of Christ. This is how we are enabled to carry out actions of love.

"Thanks to the strength of the Word of Christ, each one of us can make ourselves the brother or sister of those whom we encounter...(through) actions of closeness, actions which manifest the love that Christ taught us."[87]

...none of us lives in the flesh any more, at least not in so far as living in the flesh means being subject to the weaknesses of the flesh, which include corruptibility. Once we thought of Christ as being in the flesh, but we do not do so any longer, says St Paul. By this he meant that the Word became flesh and dwelt among us; he suffered death in the flesh in order to give all men life. It was in this flesh that we knew him before, but we do so no longer. Even though he remains in the flesh, since he came to life again on the third day and is now with his Father in heaven, we know that he has passed beyond the life of the flesh; for having died once, he will never die again, death has no power over him any more…

Since Christ has in this way become the source of life for us, we who follow in his footsteps must not think of ourselves as living in the flesh any longer, but as having passed beyond it. St Paul's saying is absolutely true that when anyone is in Christ he becomes a completely different person: his old life is over and a new life has begun. We have been justified by our faith in Christ and the power of the curse has been broken… This is all God's doing.[88]

"May our most Holy Mother help us in this, so that in each of our daily lives love of God and love of neighbour may be ever united."[89]

Challenge: "The Word became flesh to be our model of holiness". (*CCC* 458) Look up, read and pray the Beatitudes. (*Mt* 5:1-12)

THE ASCENSION OF THE LORD

Almighty God, fill us with a holy joy; teach us how to thank you with reverence and love on account of the ascension of Christ your Son. You have raised us up with him: where he, the head, has preceded us in glory, there we, the body, are called in hope. Through Christ our Lord. Amen.[90]

Today we hear the account of the Ascension into heaven from St Luke in the Acts of the Apostles, but Luke also mentions this at the end of his Gospel and although he gives a briefer account there, he includes one extra detail, that of the blessing Jesus gives. "He led them out as far as Bethany, and lifting up his hands he blessed them. While he blessed them, he parted from them, and was carried up into heaven." (*Lk* 24:50-51) His last act while still present in this manner was to bless – the blessing of a priest.[91]

Pope Francis notes the significance of this blessing:

…during the Ascension Jesus made the priestly gesture of blessing, and the disciples certainly expressed their faith with prostration, they knelt with bowed heads… Jesus is the one eternal High Priest who with his Passion passed through death and the tomb and ascended into heaven… We have One who always defends us, who defends us from the snares of (the) devil, who defends us from ourselves and from our sins... The Ascension of Jesus into heaven acquaints us with this deeply consoling reality on our journey: in Christ, true God and true man, our humanity was taken to God.[92]

The priesthood of Jesus is unique.

Although there are tens of thousands of priests in the Catholic Church, there is, in the most proper sense of the word, only one Priest, and that Priest is Jesus Christ. All other priests, however, many thousands there may be, are sharers in that one priesthood of Christ. They truly share in the priesthood of Christ, but only Christ himself has the fullness of the priesthood.[93]

So it is as Priest that Christ takes our humanity with him into heaven, into the presence of God the Father, with his hands raised in blessing for us as he departs.

Jesus Christ, the one priest of the new and eternal Covenant, "entered, not into a sanctuary made by human hands...but into heaven itself, now to appear in the presence of God on our behalf." There Christ permanently exercises his priesthood, for he "always lives to make intercession" for "those who draw near to God through him". (*CCC* 662)

The Holy Father notes another point which Luke gives in his Gospel account but not in the Acts of the Apostles; the joy with which the disciples return to Jerusalem having seen Jesus depart from them.

> St Luke says that having seen Jesus ascending into heaven, the Apostles returned to Jerusalem "with great joy". This seems to us a little odd. When we are separated from our relatives, from our friends, because of a definitive departure and, especially, death, there is usually a natural sadness in us since we will no longer see their face, no longer hear their voice, or enjoy their love, their presence. The Evangelist instead emphasises the profound joy of the Apostles.[94]

The Ascension is not primarily focused on the absence of Jesus, Pope Francis says, but that he is alive and with them in a new way. This is how the disciples were able to rejoice; through the eyes of faith they understood that they have not been abandoned; they had been blessed by Jesus as they worshipped him on the Mount of Olives, and now they are to work for his Kingdom in the strength of his presence among them in a new way.

> Jesus departs, he ascends to heaven, that is, he returns to the Father from whom he had been sent to the world. He finished his work, thus, he returns to the Father. But this does not mean a separation, for he remains for ever with us, in a new way. By his ascension, the Risen Lord draws the gaze of the Apostles – and our gaze – to

the heights of heaven to show us that the end of our journey is the Father. He himself said that he would go to prepare a place for us in heaven.[95]

This is the invitation to base our contemplation on Christ's lordship, to find in him the strength to spread the Gospel and to witness to it in everyday life: contemplation and action, *ora et labora*, as St Benedict taught, are both necessary in our life as Christians.[96]

While in heaven he is also with us; and we while on earth are with him. He is here with us by his divinity, his power and his love. We cannot be in heaven, as he is on earth, by divinity, but in him, we can be there by love… He did not leave heaven when he came down to us; nor did he withdraw from us when he went up again into heaven.[97]

Challenge: Review the structure of your Christian life. Is there a good balance between prayer and work, between gazing on the ascended Christ who blesses you and returning to 'Jerusalem' to do his work?

Seventh Sunday of Easter

Never cease, O Lord, we pray, to fill your family with divine gifts, and, through blessed Matthias's intercession for us, graciously admit us to a share in the lot of the Saints in light. Through Christ our Lord. Amen.[98]

St Matthias, of whose selection we hear today, was not originally one of the Twelve. As the time of Pentecost draws nearer, we see Peter assuming the leadership to which Jesus had appointed him and announcing that someone was needed to fill the place left by Judas Iscariot. This person must fulfil certain criteria; he must be someone who was with the Twelve from the time of John's Baptism through to the Ascension. His role will be that of a Witness to the Resurrection. These criteria are drawn up by Peter, working in his role as Pope, though not yet known as such in these early days, and the Apostles put forward two names. However, the final selection between two men is left, through the drawing of lots, to God.[99] Through this we can see the way in which the Church begins to assume her nature of a hierarchical human institution but also of her identity of the Body of Christ, fulfilling God's purposes in the world. The Apostles followed Peter's criteria and they selected the candidates, but they sought, not to impose their own preference, but to discover the will of God and align themselves to it. "And they prayed and said, 'Lord, who knows the hearts of all men, show which one of these two you have chosen to take the place in this ministry and apostleship from which Judas turned aside, to go to his own place.'" (*Ac* 1:24-25)

Pope Francis, the 265th successor of St Peter, notes that the selection of Matthias is not to do with acquiring a job, but with service.

> ...Matthias, on whom the choice falls, receives a mission which Peter defines in these words: "One of these men... must become a witness with us to his Resurrection", the Resurrection of Christ (*Ac* 1:21-23). In this way Peter sums up what it means to be part of the Twelve: it means to be a witness to Jesus's Resurrection.[100]

However, as the Holy Father points out, such service is not to be carried out in isolation, but as part of the whole mission of the Church, starting with the core of Apostles/ Bishops under Peter and going out to all nations. "Thus it is written, that the Christ should suffer and on the third day rise from the dead, and that repentance and forgiveness of sins should be preached in his name to all nations, beginning from Jerusalem. You are witnesses of these things." (*Lk* 24:26-28)

Pope Francis muses on the amazing fact that it is through the witness of these faithful men – and many others – that we have the Catholic faith available to us today.

> The Apostles had a direct and overwhelming experience of the Resurrection; they were eyewitnesses to that event. Thanks to their authoritative testimony, many people came to believe; from faith in the risen Lord, Christian communities were born and are born continually. We too, today, base our faith in the risen Lord on the witness of the Apostles, which has come down to us through the mission of the Church. Our faith is firmly linked to their testimony, as to an unbroken chain which spans the centuries, made up not only by the successors of the Apostles, but also by succeeding generations of Christians. Like the Apostles, each one of Christ's followers is called to become a witness to his Resurrection, above all in those human settings where forgetfulness of God and human disorientation are most evident.[101]

We see also from the account of this event, how the whole matter was set firmly within the context of prayer. After the Ascension, the Apostles returned to Jerusalem and to the Upper Room where they were staying. Perhaps it could be assumed that this was the same Upper Room in which Jesus consecrated them as priests and instituted the Eucharist at the Last Supper; certainly the Apostles would have felt greatly drawn to that place. And they were not alone. Praying there with them were our Blessed Lady, members of Jesus's extended family and the 'women' who had followed and cared for him as he travelled. Through prayer they were able to 'abide' in Jesus as they waited for the descent of the Holy Spirit and this prayer united them as they waited.

Pope Francis gives us this same understanding:

An essential aspect of witness to the risen Lord is unity among ourselves, his disciples, in the image of his own unity with the Father... From this eternal love between the Father and the Son, poured into our hearts through the Holy Spirit (cf. *Rm* 5:5), our mission and our fraternal communion draw strength; this love is the ever-flowing source of our joy in following the Lord... to abide in God and in his love, and thus to proclaim by our words and our lives the Resurrection of Jesus, to live in unity with one another and with charity towards all.[102]

Challenge: Pray for (or with) someone in your parish or community today who appears to find unity with others difficult.

Pentecost

Come Holy Spirit, fill the hearts of your faithful and kindle in them the fire of your love.

Send forth your Spirit and they shall be created and you shall renew the face of the earth.

O God, who by the light of the Holy Spirit did instruct the hearts of the faithful, grant that by that same Spirit we may be truly wise and ever rejoice in his consolations. Through Christ our Lord. Amen.

On this day, the Church, which had been confined to the Upper Room and to a small set of people, was opened up to the world by the descent of the Holy Spirit.

On that day, the Holy Trinity is fully revealed. Since that day, the Kingdom announced by Christ has been open to those who believe in him: in the humility of the flesh and in faith, they already share in the communion of the Holy Trinity. By his coming, which never ceases, the Holy Spirit causes the world to enter into the "last days", the time of the Church, the Kingdom already inherited though not yet consummated. (*CCC* 732)

Before the Incarnation the world knew only of God the Father, of whom the prophets spoke and to whom the Jewish people belonged. When Jesus came to live among his people, those who had ears to hear and eyes to see acknowledged Christ the Son; a huge leap of faith for a people trained for so long in monotheism. Now we live in the time of the Holy Spirit and the Church in which the Holy Spirit announces, bears witness to, makes present and spreads the mystery of our communion with the Holy Trinity. (Cf. *CCC* 738)

Pope Francis points out the universality of the Church; she is for the whole world and she bears the whole truth. The Church is Catholic, or 'whole' in a double sense; she has the "fullness of the means of salvation" and has been sent on a mission to the whole human race. (Cf. *CCC* 830-831)

...the first Christian Community, no longer closed in upon itself, begins speaking to crowds of different origins about the mighty works that God has done (cf. v. 11), that is to say, of the Resurrection of Jesus who was crucified. Each one present hears his own language being spoken by the disciples. The gift of the Holy Spirit restores the linguistic harmony that was lost in Babel, prefiguring the universal mission of the Apostles. The Church is not born isolated, she is born universal, one, and Catholic, with a precise identity, open to all, not closed, an identity which embraces the entire world, excluding no one.[103]

The Holy Father describes this new season as one of "testimony and fraternity". The sign of the vast amount of pilgrims in Jerusalem for the feasts of Pentecost being able to understand the testimony of the Apostles in their own languages demonstrates the universality of the Gospel message and the brotherhood of all those who accept it.

> The Holy Spirit at Pentecost pours into the hearts of the disciples and begins a new season: the season of testimony and fraternity. It is a season which comes from above, comes from God, like the tongues of fire that rest on the head of each disciple. It was the flame of love which burns all harshness; it was the tongue of the Gospel which surpasses manmade borders and reaches the hearts of the multitudes, without distinction of language, race or nationality. As on that day of Pentecost, the Holy Spirit is poured out constantly even today on the Church and on each one of us…[104]

This is also our mission; to hear the words of the Christ through his Apostles, to receive his grace through the liturgy and sacraments of the Church and to testify to those who have not heard or understood, through the witness of our lives, our prayers and our words. The redeeming work of Jesus Christ, Son of God, is for everyone – no one comes to the Father except through him. (Cf. *Jn* 14:6)

> All men are called to belong to the new people of God. Wherefore this people, while remaining one and only one, is to be spread throughout the whole world and

must exist in all ages, so that the decree of God's will may be fulfilled. In the beginning God made human nature one and decreed that all his children, scattered as they were, would finally be gathered together as one. It was for this purpose that God sent his Son, whom he appointed heir of all things, that be might be teacher, king and priest of all, the head of the new and universal people of the sons of God. For this too God sent the Spirit of his Son as Lord and Life-giver. He it is who brings together the whole Church and each and every one of those who believe, and who is the well-spring of their unity in the teaching of the Apostles and in fellowship, in the breaking of bread and in prayers.[105]

Come, Holy Spirit, live in us
With God the Father and the Son,
And grant us your abundant grace
To sanctify and make us one.

May mind and tongue made strong in love
Your praise throughout the world proclaim,
And may that love within our hearts
Set fire to others with its flame.

Most blessèd Trinity of love,
For whom the heart of man was made,
To you be praise in timeless song,
And everlasting homage paid.[106]

Endnotes

1 Ash Wednesday Mass.

2 Ash Wednesday, Homily of Pope Francis, Basilica of Santa Sabina, Wednesday, 18th February 2015.

3 *Didache Bible*, Ignatius Press, San Francisco, 2014, Commentary on Joel ch 2.

4 Ash Wednesday, Homily of Pope Francis, Basilica of Santa Sabina, Wednesday, 18th February 2015.

5 Ibid.

6 Ibid.

7 Office of Readings, First Sunday of Lent.

8 Pope Francis, Angelus, St Peter's Square, First Sunday of Lent, 22nd February 2015.

9 Ibid.

10 Pope Francis, Angelus, St Peter's Square, First Sunday of Lent, 9th March 2014 (my emphasis).

11 Prayer over the people at Mass, Second Sunday of Lent.

12 Pope Francis, Angelus, St Peter's Square, Second Sunday of Lent, 1st March 2015.

13 Ibid.

14 Pope Francis, Homily at a Roman parish, Sunday, 12th March 2017.

15 *CCC* 555, from the Byzantine Liturgy for the Feast of the Transfiguration.

16 Pope Francis, Angelus, St Peter's Square, Second Sunday of Lent, 1st March 2015.

17 Ibid.

18 Morning Prayer, Third Sunday of Lent.

19 Pope Francis, Angelus, St Peter's Square, Third Sunday of Lent, 8th March 2015.

20 Ibid.

21 Ibid.

22 Evening prayer, Third Sunday of Lent.

23 Opening prayer at Mass, Thursday of the Fourth week in Lent.

24 Pope Francis, Angelus, St Peter's Square, Fourth Sunday of Lent, 15th March 2015.

25 *https://twitter.com/pontifex/stat us/340354709237923840?lang= en-gb*

26 Pope Francis, Angelus, St Peter's Square, Fourth Sunday of Lent, 15th March 2015.

27 John Donne, Sermon on the Nativity, preached on the evening of Christmas Day 1624.

28 Pope Francis, Angelus, St Peter's Square, Fourth Sunday of Lent, 15th March 2015.

29 Opening prayer for Mass, Fifth Sunday of Lent.

[30] Pope Francis, General Audience, St Peter's Square, 6th August 2014.

[31] Ash Wednesday, Homily of Pope Francis, Basilica of Santa Sabina, Wednesday, 18th February 2015.

[32] St John Paul II, Encyclical *Fides et Ratio*, n. 1.

[33] Pope Francis, Angelus, St Peter's Square, Fifth Sunday of Lent, 22nd March 2015.

[34] Ibid.

[35] Opening prayer for Mass on Palm Sunday.

[36] Pope Francis, Homily at Mass, St Peter's, Palm Sunday, 2015.

[37] Pope Francis, Homily at the Casa Santa Marta Chapel, 29th November 2016.

[38] Pope Francis, Palm Sunday Homily reproduced here, *http:// www.sconews.co.uk/news/26867/ pope-francis-palm-sunday-homily/ 24th March 2013*.

[39] Opening prayer of Chrism Mass.

[40] Holy Chrism Mass, Homily of his Holiness Pope Francis Vatican Basilica, Holy Thursday, 2nd April 2015.

[41] Ibid.

[42] *Christifideles Laici*, n. 14

[43] Holy Chrism Mass, Homily of his Holiness Pope Francis, Vatican Basilica, Holy Thursday, 2nd April 2015.

[44] Gospel Acclamation, Chrism Mass.

[45] Prayer over the Offerings, Holy Thursday, Mass of the Lord's Supper.

[46] Other translations, including the one we usually hear at Mass, put the emphasis on the *perfection* of Christ's love for those who were his own.

[47] Homily of his Holiness Pope Francis, "Our Father" Church, Rebibbia New Complex District Prison, Rome, Holy Thursday, 2nd April 2015.

[48] *Didache Bible*, commentary on John 13:1.

[49] Homily of his Holiness Pope Francis, "Our Father" Church, Rebibbia New Complex District Prison, Rome, Holy Thursday, 2nd April 2015.

[50] Homily of his Holiness Pope Francis, Vatican City, Sunday, 16th August 2015.

[51] Opening prayer for the Liturgy of the Lord's Passion, Good Friday.

[52] Father Raniero Cantalamessa, Preacher of The Pontifical Household, Good Friday Homily, St Peter's Basilica, 3rd April 2015. The honour of delivering the sermon on Good Friday falls to the Preacher of the Papal Household. Pope Paul IV (1555-1559) created

the office of 'Apostolic Preacher', meaning someone designated to preach for the Pope and senior Vatican officials – in fact, the Preacher of the Papal Household (as the office is known today) is the only cleric in the Catholic Church allowed to preach to the Pope. *https://cruxnow.com/analysis/2017/04/14/popes-preacher-today-fills-singular-slot/*

[53] Prayer after the third reading at the Easter Vigil.

[54] Instruction at the start of the Easter Vigil.

[55] Homily of his Holiness Pope Francis, Vatican Basilica, Holy Saturday, 4th April 2015.

[56] Ibid.

[57] Ibid.

[58] Pope Francis, Encyclical Letter *Lumen Fidei*, n. 4.

[59] *Exultet*, Easter Vigil.

[60] Opening prayer of Mass for Easter Sunday, Mass during the day.

[61] *Urbi Et Orbi* Message of his Holiness Pope Francis, Easter 2015, Central Loggia of The Vatican Basilica, Sunday, 5th April 2015.

[62] Ibid.

[63] Easter Vigil, Homily of his Holiness Benedict XVI, St Peter's Basilica, Holy Saturday, 7th April 2012.

[64] Morning Prayer, Second Sunday of Easter.

[65] Pope Francis, Regina Cæli, St Peter's Square, Second Sunday of Easter (or Divine Mercy Sunday), 12th April 2015.

[66] Ibid.

[67] From a homily on the Gospels by Pope St Gregory the Great, Office of Readings for the Feast of St Thomas the Apostle (my emphasis).

[68] Evening Prayer, Third Sunday of Easter.

[69] Pope Francis, Regina Cæli, St Peter's Square, Third Sunday of Easter, 19th April 2015.

[70] J. L. Makenzie SJ, *Dictionary of the Bible*, article on "Witness".

[71] Pope Francis, Regina Cæli, St Peter's Square, Third Sunday of Easter, 19th April 2015.

[72] Ibid.

[73] Ibid.

[74] Opening prayer of Mass for the Fourth Sunday of Easter.

[75] Pope Francis, Regina Cæli, St Peter's Square, Fourth Sunday of Easter, 26th April 2015.

[76] Ibid.

[77] From a homily on the Gospels by Pope St Gregory the Great, given in the Office of Readings, Fourth Sunday of Easter.

[78] Pope Francis, Regina Cæli, St Peter's Square, Fourth Sunday of Easter, 26th April 2015.

[79] Opening prayer of Mass for the Fifth Sunday of Easter.

[80] Pope Francis, Regina Cæli, St Peter's Square, Fifth Sunday of Easter, 3rd May 2015.

[81] Ibid.

[82] Ibid.

[83] Ibid.

[84] Prayer after Communion, Mass for the Sixth Sunday of Easter.

[85] Pope Francis, Regina Cæli, St Peter's Square, Sixth Sunday of Easter, 10th May 2015.

[86] Ibid.

[87] Ibid.

[88] From the commentary on the second letter to the Corinthians by Bishop St Cyril of Alexandria, Office of Readings for the Sixth Sunday of Easter.

[89] Pope Francis, Regina Cæli, St Peter's Square, Sixth Sunday of Easter, 10th May 2015.

[90] Afternoon prayer, the Ascension of the Lord.

[91] It is interesting to note in pictures of the Ascension, how many do not show Christ imparting this priestly blessing but rather show him with his hands raised in a gesture of prayer.

[92] Pope Francis, General Audience, St Peter's Square, Wednesday, 17th April 2013.

[93] Austin Green OP, Article in *Homiletic and Pastoral Review*, "The Eternal Priesthood of Jesus Christ", 1st June 2012.

[94] Pope Francis, General Audience, St Peter's Square, Wednesday, 17th April 2013.

[95] Pope Francis, Regina Caeli, St Peter's Square, Sunday, 1st June 2014.

[96] Pope Francis, General Audience, St Peter's Square, Wednesday, 17th April 2013.

[97] From a sermon by St Augustine, Office of Readings, The Ascension of the Lord.

[98] Prayer after Communion, the Feast of St Matthias, Apostle.

[99] This was an accepted Jewish convention of the time.

[100] Homily of his Holiness Pope Francis, St Peter's Square, Seventh Sunday of Easter, 17th May 2015.

[101] Ibid.

[102] Ibid.

[103] Solemnity of Pentecost, Pope Francis, Regina Cæli, St Peter's Square, Sunday, 24th May 2015.

[104] Ibid.

[105] *Lumen Gentium*, n. 13.

[106] *Stanbrook Abbey Hymnal*, Terce, Feast of Pentecost.